My Pet Dog

by Jackie Walter and Ocean Hughes

FRANKLIN WATTS
LONDON•SYDNEY

Dogs need to eat.

I give my dog some food.

Dogs need to drink.

I give my dog some water.

Dogs need to walk.

I give my dog a bath.

Dogs need to play.

I give my dog a toy.

Dogs need to sleep.

I give my dog a blanket.

Talk and Explore

Ask your child to describe each picture below, in their own words, pointing to each picture in turn.

Look together at what the child does to take care of the dog.

Independent Reading

This series is designed to provide an opportunity for your child to read on their own. These notes are written for you to help your child choose a book and to read it independently.

In school, your child's teacher will often be using reading books which have been banded to support the process of learning to read. Use the book band colour your child is reading in school to help you make a good choice. *My Pet Dog* is a good choice for children reading at Red Band in their classroom to read independently.

The aim of independent reading is to read this book with ease, so that your child enjoys it and relates it to their own experiences.

About the book
This book explains how to look after a pet dog.

Before reading
Help your child to learn how to make good choices by asking: "Why did you choose this book? Why do you think you will enjoy it?" Look at the cover together and ask: "What do you think we will find out about in this book?" Talk about dogs that you or other people you know have. Ask: "Do you think all dogs will need the same things to be looked after?"

Remind your child that they can try to sound out the letters to make a word if they get stuck.

Decide together whether your child will read the book independently or read it aloud to you. When books are short, as at Red, your child may wish to do both!

During reading

If reading aloud, support your child if they hesitate or ask for help by telling the word. Remind your child of what they know and what they can do independently.

If reading to themselves, remind your child that they can come and ask for your help if stuck.

After reading

Support understanding of the book by asking your child to tell you what they found out. Did they learn anything new? Did anything surprise them?

As you discuss the different actions in the book, you might begin to use vocabulary such as bowl, lead, collar, tail.

Give your child a chance to respond to the book: "Have you ever helped take care of a dog? What did you do?"

Use the Talk and Explore activity to encourage your child to talk about what they have learned.

Extending learning

Think about other pet animals that need looking after. Do they need the same things? What different needs do different pets have?

On a few of the pages, check your child can finger point accurately by asking them to show you how they kept their place in the print by tracking from word to word.

Help your child to use letter information by asking them to find the interest word on each page by using the first letter. For example: "Which word is 'food'? How did you know it was that word?"

Franklin Watts
First published in Great Britain in 2021
by The Watts Publishing Group

Series Editors: Jackie Hamley and Melanie Palmer
Series Advisors and Development Editors: Dr Sue Bodman and Glen Franklin
Series Designers: Peter Scoulding and Cathryn Gilbert

A CIP catalogue record for this book is
available from the British Library.

ISBN 978 1 4451 7597 3 (hbk)
ISBN 978 1 4451 7596 6 (pbk)
ISBN 978 1 4451 7598 0 (library ebook)
ISBN 978 1 4451 8333 6 (ebook)

Printed in China

Franklin Watts
An imprint of
Hachette Children's Group
Part of The Watts Publishing Group
Carmelite House
50 Victoria Embankment
London EC4Y 0DZ

An Hachette UK Company
www.hachette.co.uk

www.franklinwatts.co.uk